The Northamptonshire Poetry
and Sketches
of
George Harrison
(1876-1950)

by
John and Vera Worledge

With best Wishes

Vera & John

1999

Jema Publications

Published 1996 by Jema Publications

ISBN   1-871468-48-5

Publisher's note
Every care has been taken in the preparation of this book and all the
information has been carefully checked and is believed to be correct at the
time of publication. However, neither the author or the publishers can accept
responsibility for any errors or omissions or for any loss, damage, injury or
inconvenience resulting from the use of this book.

Jema Publications
40 Ashley Lane
Moulton
Northampton
NN3 7TJ

Printed and bound in Great Britain by Woolnough Bookbinding Ltd,
Wellingborough

Contents

WANDERERS IN NORTHAMPTONSHIRE PRESENT

THE NORTHAMPTONSHIRE POETRY AND SKETCHES OF GEORGE HARRISON
by
John and Vera Worledge

After our trips around the county to bring the lovely sketches of George back to life, together with the photographs in two previous books, it seemed an ideal opportunity to share a selection of George's poems that would often accompany his sketches in the local papers. Between 1921 & 1946 he published five books of poetry. In these five books he wrote about the towns and villages around the county, relating not only to the beautiful scenes he saw but also to historical incidences.

As we toured the county taking our photographs we would sit for a while and muse over the scenes in front of us as we read his poems. Even with the mechanisation of farming today you can still relate George's scenes of the stooks of corn in the fields, to the rolls of straw we see today.

There are still little pockets of our countryside where you can go and lock yourself away from the noise and bustle of the today's world. To sit beside the Nene at Woodford and watch the heron stalk the fish, then a quick stab and a lazy sweep of the wings, heading nest-wards to feed the young. Or visit lovely Denford to feed the ducks and take a leisurely stroll along the bank of the river, turning your back on the incessant drone of traffic on the nearby A1/M1 link road. Meander through the streets of Aynho and see the apricot trees remaining from the era of the Cartwrights.

Walk into the church at Ashby St Ledgers and see the magnificent three tiered Jacobean pulpit. Stand and smell the history of the church or walk past the Manor gate house and glance up to think what evil plot Robert Catesby and friends hatched there all those years ago.

There is so much to see in this county of ours and sadly we can only show and share with you a minute part. We hope that our books have whetted your appetite to go out and look around and to find your own little paradise.
Good luck to you all.

Vera & John Worledge
September 1996

The Northamptonshire Poetry And Sketches
of
George Harrison (1876-1950)

Compiled by
John and Vera Worledge

SPONSORED BY AND DEDICATED TO

Mr. A.G. Brigstock of Kettering,
Mrs. R.H. Thompson of Wilby, in memory of her late Mother and Father,
Ernest and Annie Stanley,
The Kettering Lord Mayor's Fund,
Mr. Colin Lindsay of Northampton,
British Gas.
(Without whose help this book would not have been published.)

With Grateful Thanks to the following

Dorothy Webb, Joan Carnell & Mary Exley, the Grand-daughters of George Harrison,
Renee Goodliffe Aunty to the grand-daughters,
Malcolm Robinson of the Kettering Library Archives,
The Editors of the Kettering Leader & Telegraph & The Citizen,
Carmel Crawley, Archivist to the newspapers,
Wellingborough Libraries Archives,
Prontoprint (Northampton) for the final photostats,
The people of Northamptonshire for their outstanding help,
Northamptonshire Archives Wootton Hall.

From the beginning of this project we have said that all the profits and royalties from the book will go to the charity chosen by George's Grand Daughters for all the help they have given to us, especially during our research for our two books on George's travels around the county.

This charity is, "The Carey Baptist Church Repair Fund."

GEORGE HARRISON'S
FOREWORD
Written for his book in 1921

To the author, upon the production of his first volume, there comes a sense of timidity. He places his thoughts permanently before the public, with whom rests the final judgement of appreciation or otherwise. In poetry this is felt in a much larger degree than in prose, because the author instinctively feels that his public is limited and uncertain.

The production of these poems has been born of an intense love for the beauties of the natural world, especially in the county of Northamptonshire, and within the immediate neighbourhood of my own home in Kettering. The charm of its undulating countryside, its reedy streams and quiet woodlands, has called insistently for expression which I have endeavoured to give, not without the full consciousness of the difficulties of poetry as a means of portraying oneself, nor of the impossibility of portraying by mere words all that I feel for a world of loveliness that has given me my greatest pleasure from earliest boyhood.

My thanks are due to my friends, the Rev. T.N.Tattersall D.S.O., J.W.Smith, R. Burley Wallis J.P., A.Yates and F.Hutchen for their encouragement and appreciation extending over many years.

George Harrison 1921

A young George Harrison

Extract from the Kettering Leader dated 4th November 1921
reviews George Harrison's poetry, and is reproduced here with grateful
thanks to Malcolm Robinson of the Kettering Library Archives.

A LOCAL LYRIST
THE ART OF MR. GEORGE HARRISON
POEMS
BY
GEORGE HARRISON, KETTERING.

There is in the manner which an author gazes on his first work fresh from the publishers something akin to the mixed feelings with which a father gazes on his first-born son. Something of the same pride, the same awe and reverence. For is it not the first-born creature of his imagination, a child whose birth was the outcome of much anxious thought and labour?

And then to have to surrender it to the cold, unsympathetic eyes of the world, and wait in an agony of tension for the verdict of Public Opinion. What will the critics say, he wonders? Will they accord his work just the careless scrutiny that is apt to be the lot of most new writers, especially if they be poets. He prays that if they miss the delicate beauty lying hidden that at least they will not "damn by faint praise" in the callous way reviewers have, nor with heavy satire effect to admire the way the volume is produced but ignore the contents.

Such were the thoughts that flitted through our minds when a small volume fresh from the press, and hearing the simple title "Poems" came into our hands. It is by George Harrison, Kettering's poet-artist, and in his foreword the author confesses to a certain sense of timidity in offering his first volume to the public. But, really Mr Harrison is not in so unenviable a position as some authors, for through the medium of this and other journals he has already won an appreciative circle of admirers.

True, the mere fact of odd poems by anyone finding their way into print is no guarantee of literary merit; in fact, we are bound to admit that many of the verses that secure a place in some journals utterly fail to rise above mediocrity.

But while we should not dream of pretending that Mr Harrison's work is criticism-proof, we do say that it is far from deserving the description "mediocre." The whole of the poems included in this work are marked by symmetrical beauty, but it is not on the structure excellence of Mr Harrison's verse that we wish to dwell. The appeal of the author's work lies in the sense of restfulness that pervades the whole of the poems. He treats of the scenes we know, and reveals to us the beauties that lie unsuspected by our duller perception near at hand.

Seventy-five poems in all figure in the work, and nearly all are of what one may term the pastoral variety. But though unmarked by striking similarity, the author has contrived to picture the commonplace in such a way we love him for it. We see nature as he sees it, and incidentally we gain an insight into the mind of the man himself.

Most of the poems here enshrined have appeared from time to time in own columns; and it was the desire to give them a more permanent collective form that prompted a trio of local admirers - the Rev. T.N. Tattersall, D.S.O., Mr R.B.Wallis, J.P., and Mr. J. W.Smith to undertake the issue of the present volume.

Mr. Harrison has thus had the advantage of skilful and sympathetic editorship, resulting in a discriminating selection and a plethora of choice, and a praiseworthy arrangement which, while admirably sustaining the sequence of the seasons, displays the author's motif in all its delightful shades and variations.

The value and interest of the volume is greatly enhanced by the delightful reproduction in colour of four of Mr. Harrison's represent-active local paintings, which not only serve to illustrate another and perhaps more popular phase of his many talents, but are in reality poems in colour - the adaption of another medium through and by which he seeks to give utterance to thoughts that lie too deep for words. This combination of George Harrison's Art and Poetry opens up a vista of great charm, in which all nature-lovers may unreservedly revel. His first volume will, we doubt not, be received with a chorus of praise, as worthy to rank with the best of Northamptonshire's sweet pastoral singers.

The volume is issued to subscribers at a guinea and copies in cheaper bindings are on sale at 5/- and 3/-.

Our County

Dear County of clear winding streams,
That flow through meadows cool and sweet,
Of wooded hollows, where the gleams
Of sunlight's sheen and shadows meet.
Thy sweeping uplands fold on fold
Are changeful as the breezy skies,
Where dimpled hills for ever hold
Some tender joy, some new surprise.
Here stately rivers rise to bless
The farther counties of our isle,
To give to busy towns caress
And woo the barren fields to smile.
Thy village homesteads nestle down
'Midst flow'ring fields and lofty trees,
Where Spring-time's hedgerow's vernal gown
Yield honeyed spoil for toiling bees.
Historic years have left their trace
On stately homes, where still remain
The scars of conflict grim and base,
The sad intrigue, the bitter pain.
Thus Barnwell's mould'ring heap of stones
(The little left of castle wall)
Speak now of passing Kings and thrones,
Of greater power above them all;
And Oundle, known through all the shires
For schools by Laxton long endowed,
A home for youths who dare aspire
To seek the culture of the proud.
Dear Naseby echoes Cromwell's name,
And Rushton breathes of Tresham's skill;
Fair Fotheringhay brings forth the sigh,
As deeds of shame for ever will.
Famed Kirby, falling to decay,
Seems like a spectre from the past,
When gallants met in bright array,
Till greed and lust brought shame at last.
Each village of thy pleasant shire
Serenely speaks of Britain's power,
In fluted aisle and pointed spire,
In regal home or ancient tower.
Green lanes lie near to busy town,
With fresh, lush grass for weary feet,

Thy sweeping furrows rich and brown
Abundant yield the golden wheat.
Thy leafy byways loved by Clare,
Which Cowper sought, and Dryden praised,
Were limned by East to seem as fair
As Alpine mountain crest displays.
Let others sing of counties where
Proud rivers flow to meet the sea,
Of Northern moorlands bleak and bare,
With ceaseless wind's wild ecstasy,
But I will sing of narrow lanes,   ·
So near my home on every side,
The scent of clover after rains,
The uplands rolling like the tide,
Flat meadows set by water mills,
And little paths that winding go
Through flow'ring fields and lowland hills,
With half the green world spread below.
These, these still fill my heart's desire,
And give me all the joy I ask,
In themes of loveliness entire
To mould through life my every task.

Thy sweeping uplands fold on fold

Northampton

Dear ancient town, where through the passing years
So much to change to meet the eye appears,
The Normans built thy castle and the wall
That after Naseby were both doomed to fall,
And fire and ravage swept too soon away
Mediaeval buildings with their decay.
The churches in that dreadful day were spared,
As if a righteous providence had cared
To keep them for thy future years of peace,
What men would learn of love and love's increase;
And later men lit here their torch of flame
And bore it forth to bear an honoured name;
Bradlaugh and Labouchere, their deeds remain
As sweet as leafage after April Rain;
Here gracious Doddridge long had ministered,
And pious Rylands preached the holy word
That gave men visions of a purer world,
When freedom's flag could safely be unfurled.
Thus, through the passing years thy upward trend
Has been to praise, and with thy praise defend
The men who gave to life the pious hand
Of healing friendship to a troubled land.
Now standing here, the wistful eye can trace
The breezy upland, and the rolling space
Of meadow lands that lie beyond the town,
The new ploughed fields and fallows ochre brown,
The sleepy Nene that flows its level way
By mill and copse and hamlets old and grey.

Northampton from Hunsbury Hill

The Nene Valley

I love these meadows cool and sweet,
That lie so near to broad highway,
Where drooping pollard willows meet
And shimmer in the light of day.
I love the river flowing by
Tall flags and plumy-headed reeds
The flowers that match the hue of sky,
Those pure delights misnamed as weeds.

Here through the warm September noon
I linger idly and content,
And feel the sun a pleasant boon,
Though summer days be well nigh spent
I see the leaves to russet turn,
They flutter light as fairy wings,
The hawthorn buds with crimson burn,
Where perky robin sits and sings.

Beyond the river, gently rise
Those truant paths that winding go
By lofty trees to meet the skies,
With half the green world spread below,
Strange how the changing colours blend,
Through wooded depths and leafy lea,
With melting hues that have no end,
To glimmer like the restless sea.

Grey farms and hamlets nestle down
By labyrinths of oak and fir,
By little fields of gold and brown
Light floating films of gossamer,
That brightly beam, or fade from view
When clouds obscure the glowing sun,
With trailing shadows softly blue
Which pass away when scarce begun.

And seated here a tender joy
Comes to me sweet with odours blown,
Unfettered and without alloy,
By beauty born from beauty's throne,
And all I ask for still abides
In flowering meads, and vaulted dome,
Of tender blue where white cloud rides
Above the scenes I name my home.

Burghley House

Dear home of beauty, time does not efface
    Thy tender lines of symmetry and grace,
Thy ancient stones, mellowed by sun and storm,
    Have lovely grown in tender hue and form.
Oft as I see them sparkle in the sun,
    Like fairy things by fairy fingers spun,
The full light flushing pinnacle and tower,
    For ever changing with the changing hour,
I praise those builders who to England gave
    These homes as fair as her best sons are brave.
Within thy walls unspoiled, their lustre still
    Pure as when moulded to the master's will,
Thy works of art remain, in glory spread
    To give of honour to the faithful dead.
For these we give to thee, dear Burghley, praise,
    For thou hast guarded through the passing days
These works of inspiration, that may guide
    The minds of men to visions beautified.
Across thy lawns have passed great men and wise,
    In all that learning and of art implies;
A King has stayed to rest upon the way,
    When Southward bound, in pomp and bold array,
And Cromwell called upon the house to yield,
    Amidst the carnage of a stricken field.
Now years of gentleness and quiet peace
    Have gained for thee of loveliness, increase,
Thy fresh green lawns and fruitful gardens lie
    Serene beneath the changing English sky,
Thy noble trees that murmur to the breeze,
    Throw cooling shadows o'er the scented leas,
Where cattle stand knee-deep in plumy grass
    In sweet contentment as the moments pass
And thy fair stones in dignity repose
    Within the soil that gives the English Rose.

Here in this peaceful vale of rest,
The village nestles 'midst the trees.

Dear home of beauty, time does not efface
Thy tender lines of symmetry and grace,

Byfield

Here in this peaceful vale of rest,
The village nestles 'midst the trees,
Where erring discords scarce molest
The music of the Summer breeze.

Now mellow corn to mower yields,
Ripe berries on the hedgerows glow,
The thistledown from upland fields
Floats lazily to meads below.

Full Summer's pageantry of gold
Heralds the Autumn of the year;
In richer glory growing old
The rusts on chestnut leaves appear.

Dark purple plums hang by the wall,
In old-world orchards, to the ground
The red-cheeked apples gently fall
With little gleams, without a sound.

Above the fields a slumb'rous haze
Hangs motionless; a robin sings,
His scarlet, rounded breast ablaze,
With flash of bronze on pointed wings.

The swallows circle in the light,
Each call to each, alas, too soon
Has come the time for Southward flight
Where Summer sun is still of June.

Thus slowly to its peaceful close
Summer departs on glinting wings,
To leave behind a scent of rose
And thoughts of deep, unuttered things.

Woodford

The river lined by willow trees
Flows smoothly on its level way,
Or kissed to eddies by the breeze
Which sparkle in the light of day.
Deep through the long, cool meadow grass
The browsing cattle idly wade,
And at the noontide slowly pass
To seek the aspen's welcome shade.

Now seated here beyond the mill,
I see the changing colours flow,
The shadows in the water spill
From little clouds, that drifting go
Across the tender sky of blue,
To mirror in the river's tide,
Like little boats of magic hue,
That only fairies deign to guide.

In busy usefulness has stood
Old Woodford Mill through years of time.
The summer day's rich quietude
Is mellowed by its ceaseless rhyme
Of turning wheels and waters' whirl,
That rude fantastic shadows throw
In mystic hues that roll and curl,
And interlace and longer grow.

Through all the changing scheme of things
Woodford remains an isle of peace;
A place that woos and constant brings
A love of calm with wise increase.
When weary of the fret and care
Where carnal things my thought despoil
I know the joy that waits me there
Where I can pleasant hours beguile.

Titchmarsh

Set high upon a breezy hill,
With woods and meadows far below,
The streets look down upon the mill
And little paths that winding go
By corn fields where the poppies burn,
To roll away with curve and sweep,
Till lost in nodding leaf and fern,
And woodland shadows lush and deep.

The church, half-hid by spreading trees,
Stands stalwart through long years of time,
Each graceful line the eye doth please,
Each moss-grown stone becomes sublime
When lit with sun's departing ray,
Or when the early light of morn
Heralds the coming of the day,
Then seems each fretted stone new born.

An ancient cedar's regal form,
Through many centuries has spread
Wide arms, now seared with sun and storm,
Its early grace and glory shed.
Still Spring-time decks its crown with gold,
And makes this aged monarch seem
A thing of beauty growing old,
That age but makes the more supreme.

Old records speak of one who came
To Titchmarsh Manor for his bride,
And for a festive Christmas game
She in an old oak chest doth hide;
The rusty hinges hold her fast,
And no one hears her plaintive cries,
Until the fleeting hours have passed,
And she a bride unsuccoured, dies.

Ladies and Knights in those far days
Oft came to join the merry chase,
Across these far-flung rural ways,
With baying hounds a goodly pace.
One Robert Keyes for long did plot
With Fawkes and Winter, all were caught
And death was their unhappy lot,
With all they strove for brought to nought.

Still round each weather-beaten stone,
The memory of years remains
To murmur in an undertone
Of laughter, tears, and bitter pains,
Yet beauty lingers, now to cheer
One weary of the noise of town,
For Summer crowns the golden year,
And Summer skies bear not a frown.

The church, half-hid by speading trees.

Aldwincle

Dear village of my native shire,
    Grown lovely through the years,
Thy narrow lanes are full of grace
    When winsome Spring appears,
And budding trees and waking flowers
    Are watered with her tears.

Through thy fair meads the sleepy Nene
    Flows on its reedy way,
By bending willows, gnarled and old,
    And hawthorns white with may;
With merry fun the village youths
    In shining waters play.

Thy cottage homes (dear isles of peace),
    'Midst gardens breathe repose,
Set deep with stock and scented phlox,
    And trailing crimson rose;
The very birds sing sweeter here,
    Till day her eyelids close.

And Dryden's early home remains
    Amidst thy ancient trees;
No poet born had purer charms
    To meet his gaze than these,
Nor fuller rhyme to greet his ears
    Than this exotic breeze.

That blew across these gardens fair
    From old-world flowers in bloom,
And through the open window strayed
    Into his quiet room,
To bring the gift of precious joy,
    A breath of June perfume,

Now, when the dusk of twilight falls
    Across the fading skies,
I joy to think a poet mused,
    With loving thoughts and wise,
Among these scenes, which were the first
    To meet his waking eyes.

Barnwell

Broods here the glamour of the young May morn,
    With gentle fragrance of new unopened flowers,
The scent of apple bloom on breezes borne
    Gives added tenderness to sunny hours;
The joy of many precious things untold,
The charm of love and spring that grow not old.

Old walls before the mellow sunlight glow,
    And little lines of purple shadow cast
Across the grass, where waves of colour flow,
    That each but seems the sweeter than the last,
Until in farther fields the colours blend
In pulsing loveliness that knows no end.

Blooms now the cowslip and the dainty smock,
    The white-eyed speedwell's swimming mist of blue,
The dandelions in deeper splendour mock
    The waving buttercups' less golden hue,
And every hedgerow flaunts its wreath of may,
Soft, fairy snow-drifts in the light of day.

On Barnwell Castle shadows come and go,
    As drifting clouds obscure the glowing sun;
The trees above a moment gleam, below
    A trailing mist like gossamer is spun,
And then in fuller sunlight softly burn
The crusted stones, each dew-hung ling and fern.

And from each farm and field and long, white road,
    The sounds of traffic and of toil are heard,
And jingling milk carts with their market load,
    The call of cattle and the song of birds
Above the crude-built nests in elm trees tall,
With circling flight the rooks' unceasing call.

Slowly the children wend their way to school,
    And stoop to pluck the blossoms from the grass,
Or linger by the bridge, the waters cool
    Reflect a winsome image as they pass
Till urged to greater haste by ringing bell,
A note of warning which they know so well.

Broods here the glamour of the young May morn.

Dryden's early home remains.

Ashby St Ledgers

I wandered where the leaves of Autumn fell
  In silent splendour, to the cold, moist earth,
And Summer seemed to breathe a last farewell
  To all the garlands of her vernal birth.
Dim through the misty silence softly blue
  I saw the village nestling 'midst the trees
With moss grown roofs, and stones of quiet hue,
  Half hid by ivies spread beneath the eaves
Where Catesby lived in those romantic days
  Of plot and intrigue, which were doomed to spread
So much of sorrow through these rural ways,
  And brought but grief and mourning for the dead.
To this small room they came, those care worn men
  When chill November hung her mists afar,
And golden drooped the last leaves in the glen
  And driving rains could not their beauty mar,
They came and knew that all had come to nought
  That every scheme and hope had been in vain,
And more, for failure had been dearly bought
  And brought but suffering and bitter pain.
Still round this time-worn hamlet fondly clings
  The peace of quiet hours, that stay to bless.
The mind attune to deep unuttered things,
  That play upon the heart in sweet caress.
The ancient church stands high above the street
  Surrounded by a tender isle of green,
And bending elms, their leafless branches meet
  With glimpse of red-roofed cottages between.
Slowly an aged labourer will pass,
  Or children linger at the hour of noon;
A speckled thrush runs through the rain-soaked grass,
  Then stays to sing his simple broken tune,
And over all the grey November sky
  Seems spread in memory of feudal years,
When hunted cavaliers stole softly by
  In anguish of disloyalty and fears.
Still crimson hued the hawthorn berries glow,
  And dead leaves flutter noiseless to the ground,
Above the fields the wheeling rooks fly low,
  Then pass into the mist without a sound.

Wadenhoe

I lie in a sea of grasses,
Where the river murmurs by,
While a filmy white cloud passes
Across the vaulted sky.
Then the waving, changing colour
Ebbs like a Summer tide,
And flowers that bend to the South wind
Are little boats that ride.

I can see the road go sweeping
Through the fields and up the hill,
With the ancient church tower peeping
Above the moss-grown mill.
Here the houses and the gardens
Blend tenderly, and seem
The magic homes of far away,
Where fairies sit and dream.

The soft thistle-down floats lightly
On the river's shining face,
Gleaming for a moment brightly,
Then down the currents race.
Where the leaves from bending willows
Dip gently to the flow
Of the water, that is singing
A song of long ago.

All too soon the shades of evening
Through the meadows slowly creep,
Just a sigh the South wind breathing,
Twinkling star points peep
Through a sky of fading amber,
And brightly down the lane
The lights of Wadenhoe beam afar,
To guide me home again.

Pilton

I never walk these narrow lanes,
Nor see the fields afar,
But I can feel how lovely still
These homeland beauties are.
Sometimes the scent of April rains
Makes fragrant every breeze,
The wet grass glimmers where the sun
Strikes downwards through the trees.

Here where the little hillside dips
To meet the woodland's edge,
The cattle stand knee deep in grass
And tufts of tangled sedge;
The croaking moorhen comes and slips
Into the silent stream,
Where o'er the golden gravel bed
The wily minnows gleam.

The peaceful village stands serene,
Crowned by its ancient spire,
Which crimson sunset now has touched
With fading line of fire.
The distant woodland's sober green
Seems like a jewel set,
Enfolded in a misty sheen
Of pulsing violet.

The rising moon, a goblet, glows
Above the rim of night;
One silent star within the blue
Sheds forth its twinkling light,
The winding river softly flows
Upon its reedy way,
Reflecting faintly through the mist
The hues of passing day.

A place of quiet peace.

Oundle

Below these undulating fields, that rise
In changing contour to the breezy skies,
Dear Oundle stands a place of quiet peace,
Untroubled by the larger world's increase.
Spring weaves her garlands in each narrow lane,
With scent of leafage after April rain,
And Summer brings the pink briar-rose,
The breath of woodbine at the evening's close;
A ladened air of soft and sweet perfume,
From milk-white parsley flowers, and fragrant broom.
Here stands in splendour still the ancient school,
So wise in precept for each golden rule,
Once small in outlook, and unknown to fame,
It now has grown to bear an honoured name.
Strange that this unpretentious rural town
Should gain through art and learning great renown.
Maybe to William Laxton nurtured here,
With growing years the school became more dear,
For he of riches gave a goodly store,
That loving much, men yet may love the more
The broader outlook and the nobler life,
From knowledge gained that knows no greed or strife.
A noble line of masters laboured, strong
By wisdom blessed, to guide their youthful throng,
And youths have gone to every clime and sphere
To give to labour treasures garnered here.
Among the fragrant old-world gardens cling
More than the glamour of Spring's blossoming,
A sense of quiet peace and blissful rest
Pervades the mind unsought and unexpressed;
And backward through the years our thoughts return
To men, whose noble deeds still flame and burn
Upon the scroll of time's unfading page,
Which guides the thought of youth from age to age.
A blackbird sings, a wayward cuckoo calls,
And round earth's ev'ning tender twilight falls;
In lowland meadows phantom mists arise,
And twinkling star-points dust the fading skies;
The young May moon sheds forth her silvern light,
The sounds of toiling cease, and it is night.

Newton

So near the broad highway, yet seeming far
From human toil, thy hamlets smile between
Small winding streams, where willows are
Deep set in fields of green.

Thy cool recesses breathe of deep repose,
Engulfed by Nature's sweetly whispered theme,
With soothing tone, that softly flows
To minds that muse and dream.

Thy lonely church confined by flowering fields,
Stands a wise symbol for a cherished creed,
That lowly faith a comfort yields,
To troubled hearts indeed.

Time in his steady flight to thee has brought
But little change, save only sure decay,
That brings the deeds of man to nought,
His works to fade away.

No more thy mill wheels to the water turn,
Nor cooing doves their peaceful home survey,
Still Spring-time sees thy maples burn,
Thy hedgerows decked with may.

The ancient Romans here have left the trace
Of their rude toiling by the narrow stream,
Where king-cups flaunt their buds of grace,
And water lilies gleam.

Here from the busy town the toilers tread
Thy springing turf, and scent thy fragrant air,
And list the skylark overhead,
And pluck thy posies fair.

Long may thy rural charms and peace endure,
A green oasis near the haunts of men,
Thy fair retreats remain to lure
The thoughtful citizen.

Thy lonely church confined by flowering fields.

*With gentle sound the narrow streams caress
Thy ancient bridge.*

Geddington

Much of thy rural charm has passed away
In these thy later years; oft now heard
The roar and rush of motors through the day
To blend so strangely with the song of bird,
The sigh of falling rain among the trees,
The low of cattle and the hum of bees.

Still round thee clings the peace of age and time,
The breath of old romance from vanished years,
The scent of apple bloom, and budding thyme,
The beauties left from April's smiles and tears,
Soft drifting odours in thy narrow lanes,
When Spring fades all too soon, and Summer reigns.

Here stands thy emblem to a sainted Queen,
Who gave all that she had in life to give,
A rich reminder of the joy serene
Of sacrificing love whereby we live,
For love remains the purest gift of earth,
The source from which all noble deeds have birth.

With gentle sound the narrow streams caress
Thy ancient bridge, that faithfully has stood
Through centuries in quiet usefulness,
A trusted friend in times of storm and flood,
A tribute to the art and toil of man,
Who built for more than a life's allotted span.

Beyond the trees, where morning sunlight falls
On verdant lawns and tall ancestral trees,
Where the blithe early cuckoo ceaseless calls,
Hid by the weeping willows filigrees,
Stands the fair mansion that once housed a King,
Who hunted with a courtly gathering.

I pray thy ancient glories long will stand,
A link between the new world and the old,
Thy woods and cottages and fertile land,
And reed-fringed streams thy verdant fields enfold,
A joy for those who fain would rest awhile
Beneath the soothing calm of Nature's smile.

Weekley

When the toil of the day is over,
 And the dusk of evening falls,
When from his green enfolded cover,
 The brooding partridge calls;
There is a place where I love to linger,
 Near to the noisy, broad highway,
To watch the sun with magic finger
 Spill the last gold threads of day. ·

Pure the hue of the sunset burning
 On the trees, and on Warkton's tower,
The narrow stream that with every turning
 Silvers some leafy bower;
Flows through the meadows lush and golden,
 By the willows, and grey between,
The road-way bridge moss grown and olden
 Stands by trembling rushes green.

Flutter the moths above the grasses,
 Dim are they in the fading light,
The last faint glow of crimson passes
 Into the coming night.
Far in the North one star point beaming,
 Softly hued in the quiet sky,
On Grafton-road huge headlights gleaming
 Mark the motors flashing by.

And the eye of the June day closes
 O'er the fields and distant town;
A silver film of light reposes
 Where the winding stream flows down
To meet the full moon slowly sailing
 Into a mystic bowl of blue,
Like phantoms lost the white mists trailing
 Down the dark elm avenue.

I knew no woodlands half so sweet.

Picturesque Cottage, Weekley.

Weekley Hall Woods

Green isle, the source of all my dreams,
Of youthful joys, and simple themes
I sought so vainly to express,
In halting words of tenderness,
From early Spring and through the year
Till thy last leaf fell red and sere,
I mused and learned to love thee more
Thy brimming cup of Nature's store.
I knew where bloomed each wilding flower,
Where shadows cooled the noontide hour,
Where birds sang blithely at the morn
To greet another day new-born.
I knew no woodlands half so sweet,
Nor grass more lush for tired feet.
I wondered did the fairies play
In green recesses hid away,
Or Pan pipe forth his jocund tune
Among the rustling reeds of June.
Now older grown,
My Love remains, for I have known
Thy brooding sense of calm, thy peace
That richer grows with love's increase.
I never sought thy green retreat
When weary grown of dusty street,
But some new vision lingered there
Which stayed to greet me unaware,
A beam of sunlight streaming through
Tall trees against a sky of blue,
Or sheening mist of parsleys spread
With waving plumes, by mossy bed;
I saw the stately pheasants pass,
Bright hued across scented grass;
The blackcap swing on bramble spray,
Sing his few notes and fly away;
A butterfly would rest awhile,
To sip from flowers the honeyed spoil.
Always through sunny hours would blend
Life, song and colour without end,
To give me all the joy I need;
Full tender themes of thought indeed
That deeper grow with age and time,
And flow with full consuming rhyme.

This regal home of beauty.

Boughton House

Secluded near to broad highway
'Midst ancient trees and fertile lands,
With mossy stones grown old and grey
This regal home of beauty stands.
The hum of sure encroaching town
Breaks not its tender calm serene;
Still flows the stream o'er gravels brown,
Still sigh the bending rushes green.

Old marks remain of feudal years,
The draw-bridge and the sunken moat,
Those emblems of man's primal fears
Now happily of days remote.
The remnants of fair avenues
That "John the Planter" wisely spread,
Each Springtime flaunt their changing hues
And wave their bud points overhead.

Here shyly browse the dappled fawns,
The antlered deer and patient sheep;
When autumn hoar-frost decks the lawns,
The bay of hound sounds long and deep.
Then Reynard seeks the open fields,
To lead the pack a goodly chase,
Before he to the leader yields,
Or finds a surer hiding place.

Beneath these tall, ancestral trees
I oft-times stray through sunny hours,
Or idly lie with pensive ease
Half hid by plumed grass and flowers
To watch the sunbeams come and go,
The twinkling shadows rise and fall,
To hear the silver waters flow,
The white-throat's song, the cuckoo's call.

And all the peace comes back to me
From early years, when as a boy
I came to sketch and saw the sea
Of sheening leaves against the sky
Glimmer beneath the sun of June
Awhile the drowsy silence broods
Around the mind a pleasant boon
To change with Nature's changing moods.

Upon the market cross the letters
  Carved for a gracious queen.

St Andrew's Church, Brigstock.

Brigstock

By leafy woods, clear streams and pastures
    Far from the noise of town,
The village stands, serene and olden
    With cobbled streets and brown,
Where to the fields the carts and wagons
    Go creaking up and down.

In old-world Brigstock broods the glamour
    Of passing years and old;
Of hunting squires and gilded gallants,
    In story often told;
Of Cardigan's and Lonsdale's daring
    In days when youths were bold.

Dear cottage homes, moss-grown and mellow,
    Stand hid in gardens fair,
Or nestle down in fruitful orchards
    To greet you unaware.
The scent of lilacs born of Springtime
    Ladens the warm, moist air.

Few know the spot where dreamless sleeping,
    The Scottish soldier lies,
Years past folk said "a ghostly spectre"
    Wailed to the weeping skies,
Or walked in filmy light and chanted
    His agonising cries.

Upon the market cross the letters
    Carved for a gracious queen,
Remain to stir the mind with visions
    Of all that time has seen
Since Drake sailed west to fight and conquer
    Where none but Drake had been.

When steals the peace of Spring and sunshine
    To this sweet countryside,
When meadows glow and waters glimmer,
    I would with thee abide,
To feel the pulse of nature stirring
    And list the south wind's sigh.

The moss grown church a lonely vigil keeps.

Gretton

Deep in the dreamings of life's even flow,
Dwell tender joys that stay to haunt me so,
Sometimes of little hills that gently rise
With graceful curves to meet the glowing skies;
Sometimes of hamlets in green meadows set,
Fragrant with climbing rose and mignonette.
Oft as I wander there, or rest awhile,
Unloose the fancies and the hours beguile,
Then as I gaze across some fair retreat,
Where by the stream the drooping willows meet,
A flood of passion for my native fields
Gives me the joy for all that earth reveals,
Enfolds my mind to bring me sweet release
From fret of toil, to dream of nought but peace.
And thou, dear Gretton, set above a vale
Where broad skies sweep and fragrant airs regale,
Reveals a vision of enchantment, where
The seasons change, and changing still are fair.
Here when the breath of Springtime scents the breeze,
And stirs new life within the swaying trees,
The valley wakens to the song of birds,
The whisperings of more than uttered words;
Full Summer brings the harvest of the grass,
The scent of clover, when the wagons pass
Down little by ways to the red-roofed farm,
Till toil is ended and the twilight calm
Enfolds the valley, or the moon's pale light
Swims through the misty silence of the night.
Within the old-world village still remain
Those grim reminders of much grief and pain.
The stocks and whipping post once source of fear,
Bring now but jest to those who linger here.
From many winding streets the distant view
Of rolling upland's ever changing hue,
Is seen between tall groups of elm and fir,
With cottages and gardens sweet as myrrh.
The moss grown church a lonely vigil keeps
O'er the green mounds where evening's shadow creeps.
Here mourners come, when falls the mellow leaf,
And time has brought to pain a last relief.
Long may this isle of peaceful beauty move
The heart to adoration and of love;
The blossoms waft their sweetness to the breeze,
The winds to sigh within the budding trees.

E'en in thy ruin thou art lovely still.

Kirby Hall

Thou ancient pile, fast falling to decay,
    Thy form stands bare to driving wind and rain,
Frail ivies cling around thy walls, they sway,
    And, moaning, quiver in thy seeming pain.
E'en in thy ruin thou art lovely still,
    With graceful lines and chiselled stones, which move
The heart to mourn that thou must pass, until
    The mind is left to muse of that great love
Which first conceived and planned thy form of grace,
    Shaped thy rude stones to wistful lines and wise
Where the warm lights and shadows interlace,
    To mingle softly-hued with sunlit skies.
To thy once gilded halls fair courtiers came
    To feast, and mingle in the stately dance,
Ladies, and knights of princely pomp and fame
    Wove here their webs of pleasure and romance.
Thy courtyards echoed to the tramp of steeds,
    The bay of hounds impatient for the chase,
The laughter and the boast of former deeds
    When Reynard late had led a goodly race.
Thy stately beauty mould'ring to the dust,
    Seems now the sepulchre of one who lost
The best of life, through years of shame and lust,
    And left thee desolate to pay the cost.
Oft-times the Summer moonlight sheds her glow
    Of magic splendour on thy ancient walls,
And cadences of music softly flow
    Through broken windows to thy spacious halls,
From Philomel who sings in sad lament,
    As was her wont in garish days of yore,
When thou wert lovely in thy rich content,
    And queens would enter by thy open door.
Here unmolested hang the silken strands
    The spiders weave to glimmer in the sun,
Grim omen of the great world's shifting sands
    That nature claims again what man has won.

E'en now a mist of glinting green,
Soft framed around the blue lake's side.

Deene continued

Methinks he saw these velvet lawns,
The lapwings sweep the breezy sky;
When evening's pensive hour was nigh,
And heard the nightingale's sweet song.
The Uplands echo's back reply.

Near to these sylvan glades he died,
And dying heard the distant sound,
Of cawing pheasants take to wing,
The hunter's horn, and bay of hounds.
Stumbled his horse, worn with the chase,
And lifeless Cardigan was found.

Still muse I here in rich content,
Awhile the charming colours flow,
Across this flow'r strewn land of dreams,
With subtle charms to haunt me so.
Charms that I feel and would express
Did I the art of beauty know.

Deene

Oh! lovely Deene ! 'Tis sweet to muse
In pensive thought the hours away,
The glamour of historic years
Here seems to dwell, and through the day
My fancy weaves romantic themes
Of tilting Knights in bold array.

Dear to my heart each wilding flower,
Each gleam of gold on old stone wall;
The very birds sing sweeter here,
Persistent more the cuckoo's call,
Whose notes the leafy aisles prolong,
Till languorous calm broods over all.

E'en now a mist of glinting green,
Soft framed around the blue lake's side,
Casts mirrowed shadows, trembling
Where stately swan and heron glide,
A sky fair, measureless, where through
The vaulted depths the white clouds ride.

Half hid by tall ancestral trees,
Elm, sycamore, and giant fir,
Green labyrinths of box and ash,
With trailing leaves of gossamer,
The Church that peacefully enshrines
An English hero's sepulchre.

Last of the Cardigans, his deeds
Undimmed through all the years, remain
With memories of Russian snows,
The mighty charge, the bitter pain,
Of his "six hundred" nobly led,
Who faced their death with stern disdain.

Back to his English home he came,
A home by absence grown more dear,
Rich harmonies of rural sounds
That fell upon his waiting ear,
Were recompense for horror born,
The bitter travail of a year.

Weldon

I linger here awhile the shadows creep
    Through cool green meadows after heat of day,
The cattle browse in grasses lush and deep,
    And cawing rooks fly on their homeward way.

Now glows the sun upon the old church tower,
    On vaulted lamp, on glass that glints and gleams,
Oft in the darkness of the midnight hour,
    The toilers have been guided by its beams.

In ancient times, a forest deep and drear
    Encompassed far these fields, these gardens fair,
Where played the dappled fawn, the antlered deer,
    And unmolested roamed the timid hare.

A wand'rer lost when fell the shades of night,
    Found nought to guide him through the deep'ning gloom,
And thus a lamp he gave, a beacon light,
    To point the homeward way and quiet room.

Still in these modern days a tender charm
    Round Weldon clings, when falls the evening's close,
A wooing sense of sweet unbroken calm,
    That soothes the tired mind to rich repose.

Within the west the moon a sickle glows,
    And sounds of traffic and of toiling cease.
From somewhere near I scent the briar rose;
    The tender twilight fades, and all is peace.

The night wind stirs the leaves, a blackbird sings,
    The trees suffused within the quiet sky
Such sentinels that guard the soul of things,
    The things that Bless, and bless to satisfy.

Oft-times I sit within my quiet room,
    When storms are beating on my window pane,
And once again I scent the rose in bloom,
    As twilight deepens in a Weldon lane.

St Mary's Church, Weldon..

Where woods and pastures interlace
And drowsy red-roofed hamlets peep.

Rockingham

Oh! lovely realm of rich repose,
    Deep set in verdant fields of green,
With noble trees, and garden close,
    And dimpled hillocks dark between,
Small paths that wander where they will,
    By shadowed copse and cool recess,
Go seeking sweeter pastures still,
    Through deeper vales of loveliness.

Fair rolling uplands melt away
    To meet the ever-changing skies,
With glinting gold and silver grey,
    And hues that match a maiden's eyes.
Ah! joy to see the cloud-shades race,
    With majesty of curve and sweep,
Where woods and pastures interlace,
    And drowsy red-roofed hamlets peep.

The glamour of romantic days
    Seem here to dwell, the hunter's horn
Oft echoes through the forest maze,
    To wake sly Reynard at the morn.
Well might the traveller at rest,
    In fond imagination's eye
See queenly maid, in purple drest,
    On palfry steed ride stately by.

Dear old-world arbours breathe of peace,
    And orchards full of apple trees
Bring Autumn's fruit in full increase,
    And honeyed spoil for toiling bees,
Along the road the wagons pass
    Through sultry hours of flaming June,
With creaking loads of fragrant grass,
    Which scent the sunny hours of noon.

Oft as the Summer sun sinks low,
    And white mists in the meadows lie,
On castle walls the crimson glow
    Lingers against the dark'ning sky.
And when the solemn midnight hour
    From ivied church sounds near and far,
Stands ghostly dim that ancient tower,
    Crowned by a wistful beaming star.

Middleton

Above the valley's green domain,
The village stands, where far below
The elm trees guard the narrow lane,
And sleepy Welland's waters flow.
Through meadows deep with flowers and reeds,
The browsing cattle seek the pool,
By little winding path that leads
Through trailing shadows soft and cool.

Here on this sunny day of June
I on a grassy bank recline,
And count the hours a pleasant boon
Among the joys that now are mine,
The buttercups are pure as gold
(No miser's gold were half so fair),
The sheen upon the hillside's fold
Could be no sweeter anywhere.

Below me lie the meadow fields,
And farther still the uplands rise,
That twinkling haze but half conceals,
To bathe the scene in magic dyes,
Until a village far but seems
Within the pulsing air to float,
Like childhood's fairy land of dreams
On seas that sail a fairy boat.

I see the road to Bringhurst go
Till lost at last by lowland hill,
The little paths that wind below
That leads to time-worn water-mill.
I see the changing colours blend,
To melting gold and amethyst,
The slanting beams of light descend
To hide the fields in dancing mist.

Dear scene, thy every mood inspires
My every thought, for love of thee,
My simple longing never tires
To praise thy charms with ecstasy.

Oakley

Little Oakley

Leafy lanes and sunlit gardens
Stand by meadows cool and sweet,
Steals the fragrant scent of clover
Even to the village street,
And the wild rose and the brambles
Nodding heads of parsley meet.

In the shade of drooping willows
I have lingered through the day,
And the white road's ceaseless clangour
Seems so very far away,
Seems to murmur like the full tide,
Creeping up the narrow bay.

And the easel and the brushes
Lie neglected by my side,
While I watch on plumy grasses
Silken beams of silver ride,
And the kingcups pure and golden
Mirrored in the streamlet's tide.

Here the swallows tireless, ceaseless,
Circle in their magic flight,
Gleams the sun on wings of sable,
And on rounded breasts of white,
Swoop they down to stir the waters
To a flashing line of light.

Late the shepherd to the meadows
Plods alone to tend his sheep,
Straight and long the purple shadows
Through the wide fields slowly creep,
Wheeling rooks above the elm-trees
Call with accents low and deep.

Languid smoke from Oakley chimneys
Drifts across the saffron sky,
Blue and grey in leafy hollows
Little wreaths of white mist lie,
And the South wind through the willows
Croons a lowly lullaby.

Leafy lanes and sunlit gardens.

The Lych Gate
Benefield

I love these quiet by-ways, where the trees
Murmur through all day like summer seas;
I love the little paths that winding go
Till lost in golden cornfields spread below.

Strange, with the passing years I love the more
The peace of Nature's ever-open door,
The breath of far-flung spaces, and the free,
Full throbbing of a green world's ecstasy.

This ancient Lych Gate, symbol of repose
Between the busy world and life's long close,
Brings to the tired heart the hope of rest,
The faith, through love in One who knoweth best.

For as the Autumn of the year draws near,
Fulfilment of love's promises appear,
And in the whisper of golden grain,
I hear the echoed joy of April's tear.

The Lych Gate, Benefield

Easton on the Hill

A village set on breezy hill,
With half the green world spread below,
Where little paths wind down until
No eye can trace the way they go,
Here melts the distance in the blue
Soft haze that broods at Summer's noon,
With shadows cast in deeper hue,
Beneath the leafy trees of June.

I love these little hills that rise
Above a winding willowed stream,
That mirrors all the changing skies
And throws far back each dancing beam,
The browsing cattle seek the shade
Beneath the trees at heat of day,
Or through the narrow shallows wade,
Half-hid by swaying rushes grey.

When draws the evening to its close,
The sun-glow lingers on the hill,
With hues of amber and of rose
And trailing lines of daffodil.
The ancient church with lofty tower
Seems set to guard the silent street,
And stands the symbol of the power
Of time that passes all to fleet.

Calm calls to calm when night has come
And star points dust the quiet sky,
The weary toilers ambles home
Through mists that in the meadow lie,
Still from the meadows spread below
Steals forth the breath of many flowers,
As though they would to night bestow
The fragrance born of sunny hours.

Fotheringhay

In the glory of the morning
Shines the sun on Fotheringhay,
Gilding far the sleepy river,
And with gold the meadow way,
Where the church with tinted
windows
Flashes back the orb of day.

Here one February morning
Passed a noble queen and wise
To a death, long born of malice,
That the strong would now despise,
For the past of good or evil
From the scattered ashes rise.

But a few grey stones remaineth,
Of the castle once so fair,
Where the scaffold gaunt and sombre,
Stood a symbol of despair.
Yet it brought and end to anguish,
Brought relief from years of care.

Strange the glamour of a sadness
Lingers o'er this pleasant scene,
For the purple, dappled shadows,
Cast between the grasses green,
Seem the remnants of the pathos
From those fitful years unclean.

Rising from the misty meadows
Soars a speckled lark and sings,
With the sunlight beaming silver
Bright upon his quiv'ring wings,
Pouring out a song of triumph
Far above all earthly things.

Now the growing warmth of sunlight
Floods a wondrous earth with gold,
Giving colour, life and movement
To a scene revered and old,
Of whose acts of queen and people
Will through all the years be told.

Where the church with tinted windows
Flashes back the orb of day

Clear waters glisten and ripple
By woods that shadow their tide.

Harringworth

Here dwells the peace for the weary,
The peace that the heart endears;
It lingers far in its green retreats,
In its cottage homes and cobbled streets,
Grown sweet through the changing years.

Fair gardens lie fresh at Springtime,
The hedgerows are white with may.
In fields of summer the poppies burn,
The swinging teasels to russet turn
When autumn serene holds sway.

These meadows a wealth of harvest
Each year to the sickle yields,
The lumbering wagons slowly pass
Through all the day with scented grass,
The pride of the lowland fields.

Clear waters glisten and ripple,
By woods that shadow their tide,
They wind along by dimpling hills
That morning sunbeams with glory fills,
To melt where the blue mists hide.

The far, far sweep of the meadows
Lie fair through each season's change,
Save when the floods in their torrents pour
Wide circling eddies by cottage door,
Then dreary the fields and strange.

Through elms the church is peeping
The bells at each Sabbath morn
Sound faintly far to distant town
To leafy hollows and hilltop's crown
A message of hope new born.

When light in the west has faded,
And stars dust the quiet sky,
Still lumbering wagons slowly pass
Through meadow ways with scented grass,
The pride and the toilers' joy.

Cottingham

White clouds, and the shadows racing
   Over the flower-strewn fields,
Rich hues with their colours lacing
   Where the grass to the mower yields,
A gleam of a white road winding
   To the blue hills far away,
A murmuring spring, where the tall reeds swing,
   By the aspens tall and grey.

Stone walls with the moss grown mellow,
   Hedge rows with roses blown,
Wide pastures lands, with far below
   The little path I long have known
Winds far through the wood and meadow,
   And always a song is heard,
The whispering sweet of the wind-blown wheat,
   Or the tuneful call of bird.

Hedged round by gardens of sweetness,
   Spreading their fragrance far,
Cottages fair in their neatness,
   Where the nests of the martins are;
The streets rise up in their steepness,
   Then dip to the meadows green,
And the leafy maze where the cattle graze
   With the narrow bridge between.

Spring brings the season of pleasure,
   Serene with sunny skies,
Full Summer in richness measure
   Weaves the glamour of sweet surprise,
And Autumn all of her treasure
   Each Cottingham orchard fills,
And the golden corn in the smiling morn
   Rolls far to the sunlit hills.

The streets rise up in their steepness,
Then dip to the meadows green.

Dear cottage homes, grown mellow through the years.

Bulwick

Here in the heart of deeply wooded vales,
And little hills aglow with fragrant flowers,
I list the singing of the nightingales
Who capture all the charm from evening hours,
And Bulwick lies below a peaceful isle,
No glamour of advancing years can spoil.

I hear the cattle from the meadow low,
In answer to the sturdy herd-boy's call;
The echo of his clearly call hallo!
Resounds among the full leafed elm trees tall,
Soon homewards, lazily the cattle pass,
Halting at times to crop the scented grass.

The stately church stands dim against the sky,
In tender lines of symmetry and grace;
The evening breezes croon a lullaby
Through lofty trees, that darkly interlace.
And cast dim shadows through the narrow street
Where meadow fields and old world gardens meet.

Dear cottage homes, grown mellow through the years,
Glow softly in the fading hues of day;
One twinkling star within the sky appears,
As slowly creep the filmy mists of grey
Like phantom boats that sail a dim lagoon,
Into the silver of the rising moon.

The rumbling carts pass slowly down the lane,
And children linger at their play and sing
An oft-repeated simple old refrain,
Awhile they trip their joyous round-a-ring
Until the joyful day ends with delight,
Soft in the gloaming sounds the last "good night."

Now falls the gentle peace of evening's calm
And sounds but come to weave a magic spell
Of sweet repose, that falls with soothing balm
Around the glories that I know so well.
Still in the heart of deeply wooded vales
I list the singing of the nightingales.

Grafton Underwood

The sun and shade at Grafton
Play in the village street,
And the chestnuts and the aspens
Over the waters meet;
The old-world flowers in the gardens
The eyes of the strangers greet.

The bells from the spire at Grafton
Ring out a glad refrain,
In the hush of Sabbath's twilight,
Dim in the narrow lane
They steal like an echo, passing
To worlds where the righteous reign.

And always the fields at Grafton
Lie fragrant to the sky,
The plumy waves of the grasses
Roll when the winds pass by,
And over the trailing hedgerows
The scent of the roses lie.

The magic of June at Grafton
Dwells by the narrow streams,
In the heart of leafy woodlands,
Haunt of a poet's dreams,
Where dew threads swinging at morning,
Like gossamer glints and gleams.

And sweet are the homes of Grafton,
Mellowed with age and time,
Old walls with lilacs drooping
Flushed with the Spring's full prime,
Deep roofs through the years grown lovely
Where the aged ivies climb.

Deep roofs through the years grown lovely
Where the aged ivies climb

Sudborough

Green hills crown this peaceful village,
  With little paths that winding go
By red-roofed farms and shady woodlands,
  To dip to flowering fields below,
In vaulted sky of tender azure
  Ride filmy clouds of drifted snow.

I see the smoke from Corby chimneys
  Float lazily across the sky,
The puffs of dust on Lowick high road
  Before the breeze go drifting by,
And cornfields, streams, and wide flat meadows
  In Summer's shim'ring white heat lie.

Near cottage homes deep thatch and olden,
  By gardens close and green retreat,
O'er gravel bed stream flows smoothly,
  Where willow, elm and aspen meet.
The ancient bridge grows old in service
  For toilers from the village street.

I love these grassy hills that leave me
  High o'er the tops of ancient tree,
Where leaves below me softly whisper,
  And murmur like the restless seas,
Awhile the truant shafts of sunlight
  Weave constant changing filigrees.

Here I can lie 'midst scented clover,
  The singing lark above my head,
The passing Spring-times wealth of glory
  In Summer's lap is gaily spread,
The wild-rose sprays trail through the grasses
  With glossy bud-points gleaming red.

The joy of peace that knows no ending
  Flows from the heart of flaming June,
In greening depths on breezy hillsides,
  I hear Pan pipe his merry tune,
For life is sweet when Summer's golden,
  And earth is yet a pleasant boon.

Cransley

Dear dreamy spot, of sweet and quiet peace,
    Immune from all the far world's fret and care,
The toil and strife and pleasure's wild caprice,
    Which claim the more but are not half so fair.

Green fields enfold thee with a soft caress,
    And little streams meander where they will
By shelving bank and reed-fringed cool recess,
    Where fragrant flowers their tender fragrance spill.

To thy approach wind leafy shady lanes,
    That undulate to breezy hills and dales,
Wide trees to shield from fickle summer rains,
    And hedgerows tall to break the wanton gales.

Thy cottage gardens grace thy narrow streets,
    Serene in honeyed spoil for toiling bees,
Rich velvet lawns the patterned gold repeats,
    Of sunlight glinting through thy swaying trees.

Oft in the slumbrous hours of flaming June
    A deep, unbroken calm seems here to dwell,
Save in that mystic hour when to the moon
    Echoes the magic I know so well.

Near where thy firs stand darkling to the skies,
    Lives one who joys in music's many themes,
That subtle art that moves and glorifies
    The sounds of nature to a poet's dreams.

And to the weary and the sad at heart
    He brings the comfort of a love divine,
A love that plays in life the larger part
    To mould earth's precepts to a wise design.

Dear Cransley, may thy beauties long enfold
    Thy pleasant byways with a full increase,
That on some summer day when I am old
    I fain may rest awhile in quiet peace

Dear dreamy spot of sweet and quiet peace

A place of quiet rest and sweet repose

Thorpe Malsor

There is a grassy hillock near to Thorpe
That dips far down to meadows lush and green,
Upon its ridge a wood of larch and pine
Shields from the western sun, or stays the breeze
When the rude storms of early Springtime break.
A place of quiet rest and sweet repose
When regal Summer floods the world with gold,
For in the sultry sun glow silence broods;
And calmness sinks into the very soul.
The distant town lies like an isle of dreams,
Above the glories of a full green sea,
The smoke from furnace chimneys, drifting far,
Floats lazily across the sky of blue,
Forms into serried lines, and melts away.
The distant road, a long white ribbon, winds
By lofty elms and waving fields of grain,
By red-roofed farms and reed-fringed narrow streams,
Till lost in twinkling haze of Summer's noon.
Here in this green retreat the cuckoos call,
And ring-doves coo within its tranquil shade,
Fair Philomel at twilight's wistful hour
Stirs the far echoes with her magic voice,
And at the young Spring morn the very air
Is pulsing with a revelry of song.
No sounds of toiling ever trespass here,
Save when the shepherd seeks his scattered sheep,
Or ploughman speaks to cheer his tired team
Mounting the distant upland's purple fold.
Sometimes within the lane are faintly heard
The cries of children coming home from school,
The village church bell's chimes, the soft "Hallo"
When sturdy herd-boy calls the cattle home.
If when the day grows weary, I would dream
Of tender themes and deep unuttered things,
I leave the toiling and the dusty streets,
And seek the grassy hillock near to Thorpe.

Cranford

A village set just off the road,
With shady lanes and meadows green,
Where vans and cars with rumbling load
Through twinkling shadows pass, between
Tall elms, and hedgerows white with may,
Small cottages with gardens sweet,
And overhanging roofs of grey,
Which shield from bitter cold and heat.

I love these winding, narrow streams,
That flow beneath the willow's shade,
Through narrow bridge, then softly gleams
O'er shallow bed where cattle wade;
I love the little path that leads
Across the field about a mile,
The parsley's tall and flowering reeds,
That almost hide the broken stile.

I love the breezy tree-crowned hills,
With half the village spread below,
The light of evening time which fills
Each garden close with crimson glow,
When old stone walls to amber turn,
Between long shadows strangely blue,
And distant corn fields flame and burn,
And change with sunset's changing hue.

For joy is with me, when I muse
'Neath Cranford's trees, and all the fret
Of worldly care I seem to lose,
And for one peaceful hour forget,
For hum of bees and whirr of wings,
The gentle wind with odours blown,
Bring me the very soul of things,
The purest thoughts my mind has known.

Small cottages with gardens sweet

Pytchley

It stands on a breezy upland,
So near to the busy town,
Where the corn fields and the stubbles
To verdant fields slope down,
And the little path goes winding
Through the meadows gold and brown.

How I love the old church peeping
Through the young Spring's silver
sheen,
And the blackbird softly piping
Where late the elms grow green,
The lane with its twinkling shadows
And the glint of gold between.

I can hear the far town's murmur,
The trains as they northward go;
I can see the rolling smoke cloud
Like snow drift, ebb and flow,
Till lost in the sombre purple
Of the osier beds below.

I love the house and the gardens,
Where Channing once lived, and gave
Long years of toil and of service,
With actions strong and brave,
Moulding his purpose with wisdom,
The lives of the weary to save.

My heart will remember always,
Remember and hear again,
His voice with the note of passion
So near to the note of pain,
And accents strong and pleading
Against all things false and vain.

And oft when the glow of sunset
Grows dim o'er the busy town,
And old elms in the gloaming
Like phantoms loom and frown,
I walk where the path goes winding
Through the meadows gold and brown.

How I love the old church peeping
Through the young Spring's silver sheen.

Kettering

Set on a breezy hill, her roads slope down
By pleasant pastures, and by narrow streams,
She has no ancient walls, No Abbeys frown
Above her verdant lawns, nor morn's fair beams
Tinge with enfolding glow a Castle's crown.

Not her's the turmoil of a City's throng,
Nor green encloistered rose hung filigrees,
Where open squares the sunny hours prolong,
And silver fountains set by shady trees,
Give their coolness to the weak and strong.

Yet I have seen through sunny hours of June
Her taper spire agleam, the gentle swell
Of upland fields bathed in the heat of noon;
Her leafy flower-strewn paths I know so well,
Are still to me a joy, a pleasant boon.

And I have known the pleasure and delight,
When musing by her narrow streams I've been,
Or lying on green hillock's gentle height,
Some new found beauties I have never seen
Unfold with winsome grace before my sight.

And names our country love and cherish still,
Her well-known streets and humble ways proclaim,
Here Knibb set forth his cause with fervent will,
And Carey lit the potent torch of flame,
He carried far with praise and loving skill.

East, Nettleship, and Gotch are names that dwell
With those who strive for art and loveliness,
I joy to know that her first beauty fell
Upon their hearts, and wooed with soft caress,
To create for men a magic spell.

Always for justice, honour, and the right
Her sires have stood the freedom and the power
Were born of men who through the hours of night,
Led those who feared not through the darkest hour,
To nobler fields of learning and of light.

Often when twilight fades, and in the gloom
The twinkling lamps and furnace fires outshine,
The soil I tread seems bathed in dusky bloom
Which through my life I always love as mine
And pray it may in death enclose my tomb.

Early Morning:
The Wicksteed Park

Far in the East, a line of melting gold,
   Moves like a bird that waking, spreads its wings,
As the fair portals of the morn unfold,
   And night's dark mantle to the Westward flings,

Upon the surface of the lake a gleam
   Of silver scintillates, the breezes stir
The waters, and the little eddies beam
   With twinkling glory light as gossamer.

The swings stand idle now, no painted boat
   Moves to the music of dripping oars,
The little island seems to softly float
   Far from the purple of the shelving shores.

A bird awakes the stillness, and the light
   Broadens before the sun's exalted beams,
The soft mist rises trailing low and white,
   The surface of the tranquil water steams.

The tall pavilion pale against the sky,
   Stands like a sentinel to guard the way,
Flowers fresh with dew within the gardens vie
   With varied hues to greet the eye of day.

And wide the open country breaks to view,
   With meadow, streams, and little verdant hills,
Full trees with misty shadows strangely blue,
   Where swamp-bound water on grass distils.

Now sounds the traffic on the long white road,
   But faintly heard within this green retreat,
The milk carts passing with their townward load,
   The whir of motors in the village street.

For day has come, with all its toil and care,
   The common round, the old familiar task,
But to have viewed awhile a scene so fair
   Gives much of love, and all the joy I ask.

*The waters, and the little eddies beam
With twinkling glory light as a gossamer.*

*Ancient trees, and roses peeping,
Over moss-grown old stone walls.*

Kettering From Glendon Lane

Through trailing hedge and lofty trees
The town lies fair as Summer skies,
No sweeter view the eye can please,
Nor one that more than art implies.

Enfolded in the light of morn,
The taper spire and buildings seem
Like filmy forms, by fancy born,
Across a realm of great esteem.

And when the noontide breezes stir
The drifting clouds across the blue,
Frail tender lines of gossamer
Change with the shadows' changing hue.

Spring sees the corn fields freshly green,
The hawthorn hedges white with may,
The new leaves on the elm trees screen
The view of pit banks dark and grey.

Full Summer gives the briar rose,
Tall daisies and the swaying grass,
The parsley mounds, like drifted snows,
Bend low to let the breezes pass.

And Autumn sees the poppies burn
Through narrow fields that skirt the lane,
The night-shade beads to crimson turn,
The wagons pass with golden grain.

At evening faintly through the mist
The distant town lights twinkling beam,
With ruddy gold and amethyst
The furnace lamps and red fires gleam.

A shrieking train will pierce the gloom,
Flash like a falling meteor,
Then leave a trail of drifting bloom
Across the starlit heaven's floor.

Still in my heart, the love I own
Sinks deeper for my native town,
When gentle sounds by soft winds blown
Upon the wings of night fall down.

And I would pray, her sons may live
In courage strong, and virtue kind,
And to its honour something give
To build a town of lofty mind.

Rothwell

Rothwell ! thou ancient town by fortune's grace,
New born to progress, and to take thy place
Among the moderns where advancing man
May shape a township to a noble plan.
Still blends thy ancient lineage with the new.
And joy is ours whene'er we stay to view
The work of Tresham, and the zealous care
Thy sires have wrought to keep a place so fair,
For wise are they who have no art to give.
Yet help the art of others long to live.
These chiselled stones are echoes of the past,
Mirrors of craftsmanship that long will last,
A thing of beauty to the thoughtful mind,
Which moulds the heart to lofty themes and kind,
Those humble homes of thine for aged men.
Have been a refuge for the weary, when
The steps grow feeble as life nears its close.
And age needs blissful rest and sweet repose.
Thy ancient church, moss grown and grey with age,
Has stirred the thoughts of every humble sage,
But these old walls thy secret long will keep,
Of those beneath disturbed, yet silent sleep.
Oft as I view thee from some distant hill,
Thy gentle charms my eyes with glories fill,
Green fields and red roofed farms, and far below,
Grey groups of willow trees, and roads that go
By lofty trees, and pastures sloping down
To end by cottage gardens near the town.
Here, still remains the Rothwell as of old,
Those dear recesses set in green and gold,
Old walls, where apples mellow in the sun,
And flowers of every season deftly spun,
I pray that in thy progress nought may change
Thy ancient glories, mystic still and strange,
Nor mar the beauty from some distant hill,
Where gentle charms my eyes with splendours fill.

These chiselled stones are echoes of the past.

A brooding sense of calm seems here to dwell.

Rushton

A brooding sense of calm seems here to dwell,
Born on the breath of deep unfathomed things,
A calm that soothes me with a magic spell.
And bids my mind to soar on lightest wings.

Thus half reclining on this grassy mound,
Where Spring's first truant beams of sunlight play,
I seem to hear in every rural sound
The echo of some far romantic day.

The bells' sweet toning from the old church tower,
The low of cattle and the song of birds,
The laugh of children at the noontide hour
Bring memories of dreams not words.

Beneath the shadow of these ancient trees
Dryden, with pensive mind was wont to dream,
And hear the music of the sighing breeze,
And lisp of waters by the narrow stream.

And he who loved yon fair ancestral home,
Zealous of secrets, yet his courage lost.
When the last fitful hours of trial did come,
To gauge the honour or the bitter cost.

Rode in the chase within this wooded glen,
Through labyrinths of giant oak and fir,
Unechoed by the simple toil of men,
Or the rude clamour of a troubled year.

Time's moving finger still has left the trace
Of ancient lineage in this vale serene,
Even on chiselled stone, the tender grace
Of beauty lives beneath the mosses green.

These hoary trees immuned to Winter's blast,
Stand firmly rooted in fond mother earth,
And little twinkling lines of shadows cast
Across the sward which first produced their birth.

From overhead a lark's song ripples down,
A pheasant calls, and on the southern breeze
The scent of new stubble, ochre brown,
Bring me the joy that life is sweet with these.

Broughton

Near to the clamour of the busy town,
Where ceaseless traffic passes up and down,
The village stands along the broad highway,
With streets that lead to homesteads old and grey.
Much rural charm has vanished with the years,
Until each day some new aspect appears,
Of modern homes in staid and ordered rows,
Which stands for all the present age bestows
To rural settings, when for simple cost
No thought is stayed to count the beauty lost.
I miss the aged elms and green retreats
That cast their shadows down the narrow streets,
And hedgerows that in Spring were white with may,
And Autumn decked with flaming berries gay,
Still, from the summit of this rising hill
The distant view the eyes with glories fill,
The pasture lands slope down, then steeply rise
Where Kettering stands blue against the skies.
The furnace smoke drifts lazily away,
To blend with tender hues of golden day;
The fields lie fold on fold in sweet content
Of promise for man's future nourishment.
A broken line of pollard willows show
Where winds the narrow stream through meads below,
And to the west old Cransley Church peeps through
It's lofty elm trees, now so softly blue,
With farther still the spire of Loddington
Stands clear against the warm beams of the sun.
A white cloud passes and the colours change,
With pools of purple, sombre hued and strange,
Then sunlight follows and the fields unfold
To dimpled hills aglow with green and gold,
Until the glamour of the young spring morn
Comes to me, with a tender fragrance born,
From moist earth yielding after fresh'ing rain,
Renewed to life, relieving from winter's pain.
A cuckoo calls, a blithesome linnet sings
The same sweet music of a thousand springs;
Still up and down the broad high road
The traffic passes with its townward load.

A sylvan spot to fill a summer's day.

A white cloud passes and the colours change.

Barton Seagrave

Barton, long years ago, seemed far away,
A sylvan spot to fill a summer's day,
When I would muse beneath the changing skies,
Where nought disturbed of toil or traffic's noise,
Now modern villas, set in orderly rows,
Blend strangely where the nodding harebell blows.
A spacious park adorns its western edge,
And boats ply past the waving reeds and sedge,
Changed, yes, and changing, still a quiet steals
Around these meadows, that with joy appeals
As in those days when East, a youth, first came
To learn those simple truths that brought him fame;
He saw these trees awake from winter's sleep,
The early celandine and daisies peep
Above the grass to greet the Spring's first kiss,
The buds to crimson turn, and felt the bliss
Of love for all that gentle nature weaves,
The subtle beauty that her law achieves.
E'en now the glamour of her glories greet
The stranger passing through the shadowed street,
The scent of lilacs and laburnums move
The mind and heart to thoughts of Spring and love,
Love for the open skies and green retreats,
Where the full heart of Nature throbs and beats.
I love to linger here at daylight's close,
When sounds of toiling to sweet repose,
Beyond the distant hill the tapered spire
Stands sharply drawn against a line of fire,
Around the lake the twinkling lights appear,
Reflected in the waters like a tear,
Or jewelled stars that for a moment stay
To light with radiance the milky way,
The sound of laughter dies, the children pass
Homeward with tired steps across the grass,
The wheeling rooks their noisy clamours cease,
Calm calls to calm, and night enfolds in peace
These little hamlets, fields, and distant town,
The long white road that wanders up and down.

Burton Latimer

When but a boy, thy cobbled street
Seemed very far away,
Where flow'ring hedgerows, sloped to meet
The buttercups of May.
I stayed to muse in sweet content
Till ebbed the light of day.

But now spreads the distant town
To Barton's green domain,
And modern houses, like a frown,
Obscure each leafy lane,
It seems thy streets have nearer grown
To meet the whisp'ring grain.

I miss the elms that lined the road,
Their cooling welcome shade,
I miss the pheasants' green abode,
Where Spring's fair cavalcade
Spread eglantine and primrose pale
Through every leafy glade.

Still success crowns thy later year,
Thy streets have broader grown;
Each day some building new appears
In fields I once had known,
Serene with seas of waving grass
By wistful breezes blown.

Thy noble Church and Hall remain,
Remindful of the past,
The years of bitterness and pain,
The strife that shadows cast
Across each hamlet of a shire
Kept graceful to the last.

May future years bring rich content
To fill each heart and mind,
Each life be full and eloquent
In acts of being kind;
Each citizen by precepts prove
Their love to thee assigned.

Thy noble Church.

Rushden

A blending of the new world and the old,
In Rushden greets the stranger passing by,
Save when the hues of early morn enfold
The lowland meadows and the tranquil sky,
Or in that magic hour when coming night
Mellows the sun's last beams of fading light.

Old cottages, moss-grown with age and time,
Stand shaded still by gnarled and ancient trees,
That oft-times waken to their wonted rhyme
When Spring comes smiling on the southern breeze,
To leave the twinkling leaf buds strangely fair,
Soft points of crimson in the dancing air.

Thy joy remains, for with advancing years
Born of the freedom that thy sires have won,
A larger purpose in thy growth appears,
Which moulds a purer trust for everyone;
Fair open roads and rest beside the way,
For weary toilers at the close of day.

Now sounds the traffic in thy busy streets,
The workshops clangour and the whirr of wheels,
Where once wound shady lanes and green retreats,
Which all thy growing change but half conceals,
Green fields and hedgerows meet at every turn,
And rolling cornfields where the poppies burn.

Long may thy ancient zeal and progress move
On wider streams than yet thy dreams have known,
Thy ev'ry precept born of acts of love,
To flower in beauty, by fond beauty sown:
That future years may bless thy sure increase,
And give thee knowledge and with knowledge peace.

Isham

Long years ago, with youthful joy
 I sketched by Isham's pleasant streams,
No thought of care could then destroy
 The pleasure of my simple dreams;
I knew no willows half so fair,
 Nor winding waters half so clear,
Each wilding flower that blossomed there
 Seemed first in season to appear.

The town seemed very far away,
 Hid in the twinkling haze of noon;
When the fading eye of day
 Closed o'er a dreamy eve of June,
The noise of traffic rose and fell.
 And made the calm seem calmer still,
A calm that wove a magic spell,
 And soothed the mind with tender skill.

Today I sought my old retreat,
 And lingered by the broken stile,
And heard the willow-wren repeat
 His tender song; and down the aisle
Of mellow green leaf's glinting sheen
 I saw the wind-kissed waters stir,
And silver ripples glide between
 Soft shadows light as gossamer.

And walking home at evening's close,
 I saw the church, the ancient tower
Stood dark against a sky of rose.
 Flushed with the sun's departing power.
I saw the distant town lights gleam,
 The meadows blurred with rising mist,
And passing motors twinkling beam
 With crimson, gold, and amethyst.

And silver ripples glide between
Soft shadows light as gossamer.

St Peter's Church, Isham.

Orlingbury

Far from the noise of the highway,
Undisturbed through the changing years,
The village nestles old and grey
By wooded fields, when Spring appears
To giant elm and stately pine,
A new found loveliness returns
To sheltered nooks, where daisies shine,
And maple's stem with crimson burns.

The children play at the noontide,
In young fresh grass of the green,
On winding paths the shadows ride,
With a glimmer of gold between,
In tender mauve and melting blue,
And undulations fold on fold,
The valley lies in changing hue
Of fields and wood and rising wold.

Here where the tall trees interlace
In the glory of Summer's prime,
The South wind fans with tender grace
The parsley heads and scented thyme;
And drifting far by green retreats
By drowsy hillsides sweet and fair,
It lingers in the village streets
To leave a fragrant odour there.

Recumbent, carved in heavy stone,
Batsaddle in the old church lies,
He fought the wolf, the last, alone,
Beneath the burning summer skies,
Heated and sore, he stooped to drink
From stream that winds through meadows wide,
Then sank beside the flowering brink
And, weary with exhaustion, died.

Little Harrowden

No regal beauty thou canst claim,
No path that leads to stately hall,
Thy simple heritage to fame
Seems in thy county least of all.

Yet I have seen the Spring return
To woods so near thy narrow street;
The sunlight beam on ling and fern
In leafy by-ways cool and sweet.

Thy church through centuries has stood,
A symbol set to guide the mind
To every precept pure and good,
In all the art of being kind.

Thy ancient Norman tower looks down
On pastures rolling far and wide,
On roads that lead to busy town
And cornfields waving like the tide.

Thus simple joys bring recompense
For nobler scenes by others known,
The sigh of peaceful reverence
For love of fragrant odours blown,

From clovers nodding to the breeze,
The quiet calm at evening's close,
When scarce the soft wind stirs the trees,
Or lifts the petals of the rose.

Thy ancient Norman tower looks down
On pastures rolling far and wide.

Great Harrowden

A place to linger and dream
      In the heat of the full June day,
When meadows and uplands gleam,
      And the white road melts away,
Till lost in the misty green
      Where the sleek red cattle stray.

Perched high on a breezy hill,
      With the sweep of the fields below,
The bountiful colours spill,
      And the mystic hues o'erflow,
To blend in a vale of peace
      And the joy that all may know.

Old cottages breathe of rest
      From the fret of the great world's care;
Warm thatch by the moss caressed,
      That the years have made more fair;
The seasons of storm and change
      Add a charm of beauties rare.

Here would I stay till the noon
      And the tremulous heat has flown,
Then sweet are the airs of June,
      That the soft south winds have blown
Through seas of fragrance and bloom,
      And the depths of things unknown.

The sun in the west sinks low,
      And the shades of the twilight creep
Through meadows and vales below,
      Where the fresh young corn fields sweep;
Soft gold in a fading sky,
      And the first fair star points peep.

Still a lonely blackbird sings,
      And the notes of his song enthrall,
The joys of unfathomed things
      On the mind receptive fall;
The visions of things beyond
      With a sure insistence call.

Old cottages breathe of rest
  From the fret of the great world's care.

Walgrave lies an isle of peace.

Walgrave

Far from the noise of the highway
    The village stands serene,
Enfolded wide on every side
    By pastures lush and green,
In spring the birds hold revel here
    Amidst the silver sheen.

Full Summer decks her paths with flowers,
    Her gardens scent the breeze,
The fragrant stocks and tinted phlox
    Are spoil for toiling bees,
No trailing hedgerow that I know
    Give sweeter shade than these.

So much of rural joy remains
    Within these narrow streets,
The clustered vine and stately pine
    Set near to green retreats,
Lead far to depths where nature's heart
    In freedom throbs and beats.

Here all the peace comes back to me,
    As in those youthful days,
When seated here, I saw appear
    The pinky almond sprays,
And heard the blackbirds pipe at eve
    Their jocund roundelays.

Oft at the evening's close, the moon
    Sheds forth her silvern light,
And dusted through a sky of blue
    The star-points glimmer bright,
As tranquil peacefulness enfolds
    The sultry Summer night.

And Walgrave lies an isle of peace,
    Far from the fret and care
Of all the discords that disturb
    To make the day less fair,
From somewhere near a night-bird's song
    Floats on the tranquil air.

Irchester

No glamour of a rich, romantic past
Pervades thy pleasant paths, thy winding streets,
No stately towers their tender shadows cast
On ancient courtyards or green retreats,
Yet round thy cottage homes sweet peace abides,
Grown lovely through the passing years of time,
Where deep in crannied walls the lichen hides,
The varied ivies cling and roses climb.

Still more of rural ways than busy town
Thy tended fields and fallows ochre brown
Give full abundance of earth's golden grain,
And near to these the traffic and the noise
Of moving wheels (dim sounds that have no end)
The call of children and the newsboy's cries
With song-birds singing at the twilight blend.

From thy now ancient Church each Sabbath morn,
Across the fields and through the lofty trees,
The dulcet music of thy bells is borne,
With changing cadence on the gentle breeze,
While far away the mystic colours flow,
Through twinkling haze o'er meadows fold on fold,
Till lost in magic hues, that men may know
Of that great love which never groweth old.

Wellingborough

To thee the flowing years have brought
So many prospects new and strange,
New hopes maybe have come to nought,
Through all thy toil of fret and change;
Still round thee clings the memory
Of men who fought in freedom's name,
And those who joyed in ecstacy
To give the truth a brighter flame.

Dear ancient homes and stones remain,
Dim echoes of the fitful past,
The shadows of bitter pain
That seething storms of battle cast,
And cloistered in a green retreat
Thy church each passing age defies,
And points above the busy street
Its symbol to the changing skies.

Viewed from some distant breezy hill,
With pleasant pastures spread below,
With here and there a farm, a mill,
A remnant of the long ago,
The town lies like an isle of dreams,
Beyond a tree-fringed cool recess,
Where every farther stage but seems
A sweeter vale of loveliness.

Swanspool, Wellingborough.

May long thy sweet suburban ways
Remain through peaceful years and kind;
Thy thoughts through life's entangled maze
Be wise by lofty minds designed,
Then shall the passing years proclaim
The birthplace of each noble son,
Who, striving still, may justly claim
To build on truths their sires have won.

Dear ancient homes and stones remain.

Ecton

The blush of evening on an old church tower,
That smoothes the rugged stones to tender grace,
And gives a touch of magic to an hour
Where lines of gold and shadow interlace
With gentleness, until the colours blend
In changing hues that seem to have no end.

I hear the distant traffic ebb and flow,
The cry of children playing in the lane;
From distant meadows browsing cattle low,
And jingling carts pass on their homeward way.
The light wind stirs the leaves, and through the grass
The little truant waves of sunlight pass.

The colours linger, where in peaceful sleep
The aged toilers of the village lie,
The lofty elms a lonely vigil keep,
And croon a vesper to the fading sky.
From somewhere near a wayward throstle sings,
And tender calm broods at the soul of things.

Slowly the twilight deepens, and the hour
Is full of memories and thoughts that move
The mind to dwell on deeds of truth and power
And all that men have proved by acts of love;
This ancient church remains an isle of peace
Amidst the travail of world's increase.

The pale moon rises, flooding distant fields
With soft effulgence. Soon the twilight gloom
Before her growing brightness gently yields,
To leave the meads, dim seas of swimming bloom,
Where grey mists rise and little hamlets seem
The floating phantoms of a poet's dream.

And dim against the sky this ancient pile
Stands like a sentinel to guard the night,
A sentinel no age can e'er despoil,
For love remains the balm for every need
The star to guide in ev'ry word and deed.

The blush of evening on an old church tower.

With meadow fields that melt away
To meet the uplands, gold and brown.

Great Doddington

A village set beyond the grey
Dull monotone of busy town,
With meadow fields that melt away
To meet the uplands, gold and brown.
The river flows by reeds and flowers,
By garden close and ancient mill,
Its music marks the toiling hours
When o'er the wheel the waters spill
With glint of foam and flash of spray
That throw far back the light of day.

These cottages serene and old
Look down on pasture sweeping wide,
With undulations fold on fold,
And woodlands rolling like the tide,
With here and there a village set
Amidst the trees, where ebb and flow
Soft films of gold and violet,
Rich, tender hues that come and go,
And glimmer like a magic glass
When glows the sun or shadows pass.

An ancient church stands through the years,
Defying age, decay and time.
Its every stone the heart endears
To all that makes our love sublime.
Here early masons left their sign,
And pilgrims touched the symbolled cross;
The sad heart still seek the shrine
For balm to heal earth's bitter loss;
The Bible chained remains to prove
The source of all abiding love.

It seems, awhile I linger here,
That toiling town lies far away,
Until the loaded cars appear,
And voices strange sound through the day.
Ah! then I know that change has come
To every rural green retreat,
That garden close and cottage home
Seem strangers in their native street,
And oft I wonder will the peace
Of life remain with world's increase.

Earls Barton

Dear town, that through the years hath grown
From village streets and rural ways,
To broader roads that scarce are known
To dwellers of those early days,
Who, turning homewards, miss the view
Of little fields, that wandered down
To flowering meadows sweet and new,
Till lost within the busy town.

They miss the elms that once did meet
By hawthorn hedgerows, near the road;
The hayricks set by narrow street;
The trundling carts with scented load,
The blackbird in the orchard close
Who piped each eve his pleasant tune,
Till twilight brought to earth repose
And closed with sleep the eye of June.

Yet beauty with thy growth remains,
So very near thy noise and toil;
Dear winding paths by shady lanes,
That lie in distance scarce a mile,
And father still the uplands rise
With half the green world spread below,
Where sweep the changing English skies,
And pure unfettered breezes blow.

Thy church remains an isle of peace
Amidst the years of fret and care,
A resting place that brings release
When sorrow's pain brings gaunt despair.
Here pink tipped daisies star the grass
And summer weaves her wreath of flowers,
And shadows mark the days that pass,
From Autumn's gold to Winter hours.

A resting place that brings release.

Mears Ashby

Now golden Autumn crowns the year,
And maple leaves to crimson turn;
On bracken fronds the rust appear,
That drooping earthwards beam and burn.
The village, nestling 'midst the trees,
Seems like a promised land of dreams,
Where naught of discord can displease
A mind attuned to lofty themes.

In mellow orchards apples glow,
With crimson cheeks turned to the sun,
And plum trees twisted shadows throw
Across the grass, where lightly spun
Hang swinging webs of gossamer,
With here and there a ling'ring flower
Which still remains to register
The glory of sweet Summer's hour.

The blissful peace of age and time
Dwells in these meads and green retreats;
The glamour of an old-world rhyme
Seems throbbing in the narrow streets;
The church perched high on grassy hill,
Looks down on cornfields spread below,
With paths that wander where they will
And elm trees set in stately row.

And now when Autumn crowns the year,
With Spring's sweet promises fulfilled,
Where April shed a silent tear
Which fragrant on the air distilled,
The joy of winsome loveliness
Twines tenderly around the heart,
As though from Summer's warm caress
The fruitful earth were loath to part.

The joy of winsome loveliness.

Brixworth

A blending of the new world and the old
    In Brixworth dwells, beyond the narrow streets,
The leafy woods the rising fields enfold
    With rural by-ways, set by green retreats.
When breezy winds of March foretell the Spring,
    And scudding clouds race far across the sky,
The lowland shadows swiftly take to wing,
    Where soon a gleam of sunlight hurries by,
And thus the changing colours ebb and flow
    With gold of field and blue of deep recess,
Which softly change to hues that none may know
    Their names, but only praise their loveliness.
Sometimes the evening with unruffled brow
    Lingers above the church in quiet peace,
As though she would to every stone endow
    A richer beauty as the years increase,
When morning floods the earth with searching beams,
    And to the west the dark clouds roll away,
Then from the church each coloured window gleams.
    And throws far back the image of the day.
For centuries this noble church has stood,
    Since Saxon workmen shaped with cunning care
Its graceful lines, from primal stone and wood,
    To leave an image rich and wondrous fair.
Still other minds and hands have shaped its form,
    Adding through passing years their mead of joy,
Set strong to stand against the heat and storm,
    It still remains of joy without alloy.
Strange that the stones left by Caesar's race
    Should be a part enshrined on holy ground,
To be a witness for the Man of Grace,
    And hope for those beneath each grassy mound.
Now when rude winter chills the passing hours,
    And shakes her frosty pinions in the air,
When scarce one sheltered spot can shield the flowers
    That made October's sunny days more fair;
A quiet beauty lingers in the lane,
    In old world gardens and in lowland fields;
A shaft of sunlight glimmers through the rain,
    Before the fresh'ning wind the grey mist yields.

Sometimes the evening with unruffled brow
Lingers above the church in quiet peace.

Castle Ashby

Dear village of my native shire,
Thy beauty still remains,
In pleasant fields and reedy streams
That flow by shady lanes,
And gleam in flowering meads, that seem
The sweeter after rains.

The echo of romantic years
Within thy gardens dwell,
Set round by velvet lawns that long
The Comptons loved so well,
With seas of bloom and sweet perfume,
That charm with magic spell.

Thy cottage homes in peace look down
On valleys rolling wide,
With drowsy woodland's wistful hues
That change like Summer's tide,
With far above the skies' fair sweep
Where white clouds stately ride.

I mourn that change on change must come
To many isles of peace,
And much of rural charm must pass
Before the world's increase,
That song of birds and quiet words
Amidst earth's discords cease.

Yet when the Autumn of the year
In fullness nears its close,
And in the twilight of the West
Still beams a blush of rose.
Then round earth's sweet suburban ways
Steals forth a rich repose.

And thou dear village of my shire,
Of all the shires the best,
So long thy pleasant fields remain,
Thy sons will name thee blest,
And every evening's calm will bring
To weary toilers rest.

Heyford

Here 'neath the shadow of the old church tower,
  When sounds of toiling cease at evening's hour,
I lingered (for the year was at Spring)
  And heard the first soft south winds murmuring.
Through budding trees and through the lush cool grass,
  That gleams and glistens when the sunbeams pass.
Spring follows Spring, yet still this ancient pile
  Looks down upon this green sequestered isle,
Through changing seasons and ceaseless rhyme
  Of footsteps passing with the years of time;
Here children come to pick the flowers or play,
  Reach their allotted span and pass away.
The very trees have with the church grown old,
  That now the sun's last gentle rays enfold.
A blackbird pipes his old familiar tune
  That blends so sweetly with the wind's low croon;
They rise and fall and gently seeming flow,
  Like wistful memories of long ago.
It may be in the years of life long past,
  When builders traced the graceful lines still cast
Upon this rugged tower, they heard the song
  Of blackbird piping, while the shadows long
Trailed through the grass, when year was at the Spring,
  And south winds through the trees were murmuring;
They caught the beauty of the things of earth
  From which all loveliness receives its birth,
And fired with potent joy they zealous strove
  To raise an image to the Man of Love.
The light fades, and the hues of twilight blend
  In quiet peace, as if they would descend
To calm the clamour of our human strife,
  Unnoticed in the busy haunts of life.
Still from the aged elm a throstle sings,
  And round the heart a haunting glamour clings
To bring sweet thoughts of beauty loved and known,
  Born on the breath of Springtime's odours, blown
From green recesses to the dusty street
  That night with calmness may be more complete.

Newnham

Set high on a breezy hill,
With half the green world spread below,
The Newnham cottages look down
On little paths that winding go
By beechen woods, and fields that rise
To meet the far cloud's crown of snow.

Here, when the winds of March return,
To chase old Winter's frown away,
The eye can trace for rolling miles
The sunlight's sheen and shadows' play,
Until the changing colours blend,
Or mingle with the hues of day.

The new ploughed furrows wet with rain
Shew twinkling lines of gleaming gold,
Then softly sweet the shadows come
Across the hillside's sweeping fold,
And standing sombre-hued and strange
A group of aspens bent and old.

I love to linger here and breathe
The fragrance born of April rain,
Awhile the blackbird pipes a tune
That echoes in the narrow lane,
And hear the brooding partridge call
That greets me from his green domain.

St Michael and All Angels, Newnham.

Sulgrave Manor

Dear ancient home, unspoiled by age and time,
    Thy hallowed name each passing year remains,
A shrine of beauty that with grace sublime
    Twines round a nation's heart its golden chains.

Among the flowering fields and grassy meads
    The scions of a noble race would roam,
Unmindful then of those historic deeds
    That came to bless them and exalt their home.

And later one of thoughtful mien and kind,
    The precept learned to only truth obey,
A precept that enriched his heart and mind
    And proved his armour on life's upward way.

Now standing here beneath thy elm tree's shade,
    As little twinkling sunbeams come and go,
I feel the spell that truth for ever laid,
    Upon the stream of life's unceasing flow.

Two nations blessed through thy sweet home of peace,
    Have joined in friendship, learning, and in art,
Each pledged to each to serve their youth's increase,
    Schooled strong for life to play the nobler part.

And as the sunbeams fade, and shadows creep
    Across thy mossy stones and gardens fair,
I know that thou a people's love will keep
    For one who made their cause his tender care.

Dear ancient home, unspoiled by age and time.

The New Year

Here, gently borne to me the joyful sounds
Of Warkton Church bells ringing. Dimly glow
The patient stars, and tranquil peace abounds
To bless the passing hours, that softly flow
Into eternity of vanished time,
That beats with measured tread its ceaseless rhyme.

I gaze afar, awhile the deep repose
Of night's unfathomed calm steals over me
Like fragrant odours of a dew-drenched rose,
Or scent of brine born of the open sea;
A dreamy consciousness of thoughts that dwell
Among the treasured things I love so well.

Is it the sound of bells that brings to me
The rich full promise of a world new born?
All passion gone, the nations pure and free,
Greeting the coming of the new day's morn,
That heralds forth the hope of love and peace
To bring the harmony of faith's increase.

For nought but love can frame the world anew,
And bring the healing balm to soothe our pain,
Endow with courage faithful men and true
Their noblest aspirations to attain,
Give to the lowly born sweet hope and trust,
And save mankind from petty strife and lust.

Ring forth, sweet bells, thy message to the world,
Ring out the hope for all mankind to share,
That never more the war flags be unfurled
Within a world where all is bright and fair,
But all nations with pure concord move
Towards the goal of universal love.

Tranquil peace abounds.